At Home
in the
CORAL REEF

by Katy Muzik
Illustrated by Katherine Brown-Wing

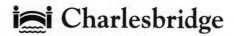 Charlesbridge

Down
down down
in the
tropical clear blue sea lives a
beautiful coral reef.

The coral reef is a wonderful
home for hundreds of kinds of
fish and thousands of other kinds
of creatures.

The reef itself is made of zillions
of tiny animals called coral polyps.

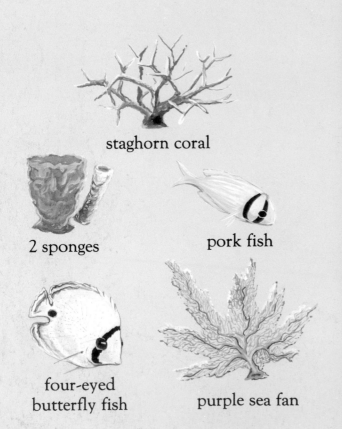

staghorn coral

2 sponges

pork fish

four-eyed
butterfly fish

purple sea fan

Each tiny coral polyp catches food with its little arms, called tentacles. The polyps share their food and live so close together that their skeletons are connected.

Some kinds of coral polyps make soft skeletons that sway gently back and forth in the water. These polyps have 8 tentacles.

Other coral polyps make skeletons that are as hard as rock. Their hard skeletons form the coral reef. A hard coral polyp has 12, or 24, or 48, or more tentacles!

Together, over 50 kinds of hard coral form this reef in the Caribbean Sea.

neon goby

spotted drum

4 staghorn
coral polyps
(hard coral)

sea whip coral
(soft coral)

What are these pink things?

Coral eggs! Once a year, coral polyps have babies. Eggs and sperm pop out of the polyps and float up and up and up to the top of the blue sea. There each fertilized egg becomes a baby coral called a planula. Now it is ready to search for a new home.

The planula is completely covered with little hairs. It swims by waving them through the water, but it cannot swim very fast.

Watch out, little planula! Watch out for those hungry wrasses!

Whoosh! Just in time, a big wave carries the planula away to . . .

coral egg   planula

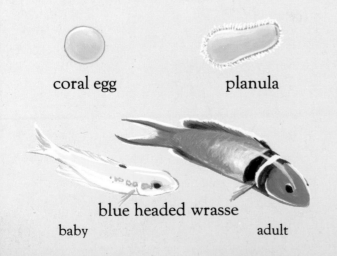

blue headed wrasse

baby   adult

the crest, or top, of the coral reef.

Here the water is very shallow. Because it is so shallow, the waves break and crash into the reef.

Splash! Crash! The breaking waves make the water very rough. It's so rough that only a few animals can live here. A fireworm holds on tight. A school of blue tangs darts in and out, hunting for food.

Crash! Splash! Will this be home for the planula? No, it's too rough. The planula is swept along, riding a wave over the crest to . . .

elkhorn coral

barracuda

adult

baby

blue tangs

bristleworm

the lagoon.

The water in the lagoon is calm. Although the lagoon seems peaceful, it is really a busy place, from top

to

bottom.

At the top, a pelican gulps a pouchful of fish. At the bottom, a stingray slurps up shrimp.

Many animals looking for food in the lagoon are hard to see. An emerald clingfish hides on a blade of turtle grass. Clams and crabs hide in the sand.

Such a busy place, day and . . .

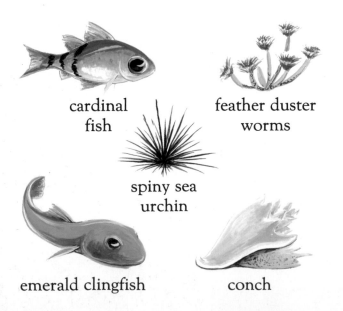

cardinal
fish

feather duster
worms

spiny sea
urchin

emerald clingfish

conch

night in the lagoon.

Flash! Glow! Blink! What could these lights be? They twinkle like stars in the sky, but they are all under water!

These lights are made by animals. Animals almost too small to see are twinkling. Brittle stars flash to scare away lobsters and crabs. Worms glow to show other worms where they are. Flashlight fish attract their food by blinking.

Can the planula live here? No, it is too sandy. The planula needs a rocky place. It floats along to . . .

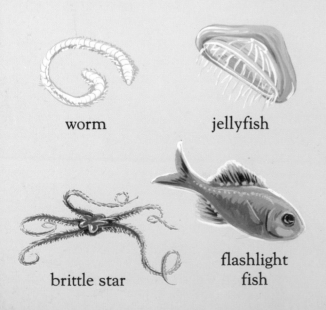

worm

jellyfish

brittle star

flashlight
fish

the red mangrove trees near the shore of the lagoon.

Red mangroves can grow in salty water. Their roots grow out and hang down right into the ocean. Sponges and seaweeds grow on the roots.

Millions of baby fish and baby shrimp start life in the water around mangrove roots. There's lots of food for them there.

Will this be a home for the planula, too? No, the water here is too shady for the planula. It turns away and swims along to . . .

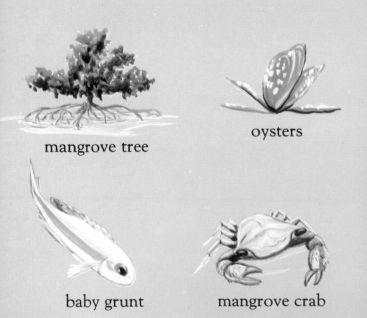

mangrove tree

oysters

baby grunt

mangrove crab

the shallow water near the beach of the lagoon.

The sunshine heats the sandy beach. The sand was made by the ocean waves. Over thousands of years, the waves have pounded the skeletons of reef animals and plants into smaller and smaller bits. Eventually, the bits formed so many grains of sand that they covered the bottom of the lagoon and washed up on shore to make a beach.

Will this be home for the planula? No, it's too shallow and too hot here. The planula catches a current to . . .

sea urchin and spine

halimeda plant

bits of sand

flaming tongue
snail

staghorn coral
skeleton

deeper water. Oh no, the water is dirty!

The water is so dirty, the coral is dying. The dirt smothers the coral polyps and blocks the sunlight they need.

Chemicals washed down the rivers from factories and farms poison the coral. In the dirty water harmful bacteria grow over the coral and kill it. Careless divers hurt the coral too. They step on it and break it with their boat anchors.

Without living coral, the fish and other animals will leave. The planula cannot live here either. Luckily, a current carries it out of the lagoon, over the top of the reef, and down . . .

Nassau grouper

black band bacteria
on brain coral

slimy bacteria

the other side of the reef
deeper
and deeper
and deeper
to a healthy part of the reef.

At last! A safe spot for the
planula to settle down. The spot
is hard and rocky. It's sunny but
not too hot. Gentle currents
bring clean water, and plenty of
food.

It will be a perfect home!

manta ray

squid

close-up of a
star coral polyp hiding

Christmas tree
worm

Surprise! The planula is changing. First, it sticks itself to a safe spot. Then, around its mouth it grows twelve little tentacles. Now it is a polyp. It looks like a flower, but it really is an animal.

Under its soft body, the polyp starts to grow a hard white skeleton. In a few weeks it makes another tiny polyp exactly like itself. The polyps are connected to each other. Together, the two polyps have twenty-four tentacles for catching food.

Oh, a little copepod! Catch it!

copepod

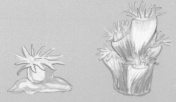

1 month   6 months   1 year

a planula grows up

The planula is growing up to be a staghorn coral. More polyps grow, and more and more.

Here comes a reef butterfly fish. It eats coral. Quick, tiny polyps, hide!

The coral polyps warn each other of danger. Quick as a wink, they hug their tentacles in. They hide their soft bodies down inside their hard white skeleton.

When the danger is past, the coral polyps slowly come out and open up their tentacles again.

staghorn coral
2 years old

feather star

giant sea fan

sea squirts

Many creatures in the reef are partners that help each other hide or find food. A crab hides in the coral to escape from a hungry octopus. A shrimp lives safely inside a vase sponge.

At a cleaning station, gobies eat what they clean from the teeth of a big grouper. The grouper holds its mouth wide open for the gobies. Away from the station, the grouper would eat gobies!

Even the tiny polyps have partners. The polyps get special food from little golden plants living just inside their skin. In return, the plants get a home. This partnership helps the coral grow big enough to form reefs.

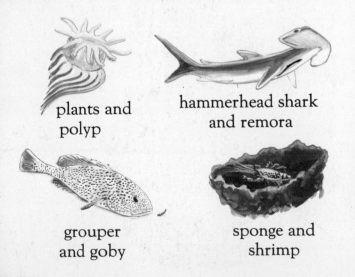

plants and polyp

hammerhead shark and remora

grouper and goby

sponge and shrimp

D o w n
d o w n d o w n in the
tropical clear blue sea, this coral
reef is alive and well. The place
where it lives is clean. Zillions of
coral animals have been adding
their skeletons to the reef for
over 8,000 years.

It takes thousands of years for a
reef to grow but only a few years
for one to be destroyed! This reef
and other coral reefs all around
the world are in danger because
the oceans are becoming dirty.
Coral reefs need our help.

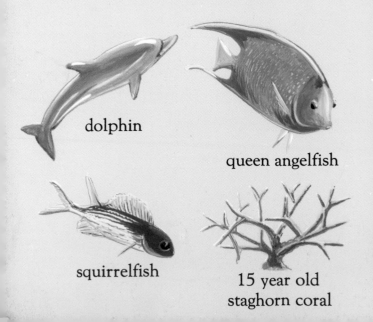

dolphin

queen angelfish

squirrelfish

15 year old
staghorn coral

What can we do to help a little baby planula grow up to become part of a big coral reef? The first step is to discover how what we do on land affects life in the sea.

All living creatures — including corals and people — need clean water. We all use water on our farms, in our suburbs, and in our cities. We throw many things into it that make it dirty. This dirty water flows into rivers, lakes, and underground streams, and eventually ends up in the sea. There it hurts the coral reef and all the creatures that make it their home.

But we can make a difference. We can make our rivers and lakes and oceans clean again. We can learn about life on the coral reef and share what we learn. We can help people everywhere to care about the amazing reefs and the tiny coral animals that build them.

To the Water. *K.M.*
For Susan D. Gibbs and my husband Stephen. *K.B-W.*

Published by Charlesbridge
85 Main Street, Watertown, MA 02472
(617) 926-0329
www.charlesbridge.com

Library of Congress Cataloging-in-Publication Data
Muzik, Katy.
    At Home in the Coral Reef / by Katy Muzik; Katherine Brown-Wing, illustrator.
        p.   cm.
    Summary: Down in the tropical sea lives a beautiful coral reef, home to a world
of fish and other creatures.
ISBN-13: 978-0-88106-487-2; ISBN-10: 0-88106-487-4 (reinforced for library use)
ISBN-13: 978-0-88106-486-5; ISBN: 0-88106-486-6 (softcover)
1. Oceans-Juvenile Literature. 2. English Language-Juvenile Literature.
[1. Oceans. 2. Coral Reef ecology.] I. Brown-Wing, Katherine, ill. II. Title.
574.5   92-70577
                                                          CIP
                                                          AC

Printed in Korea
(hc) 10   9   8   7   6   5   4   3   2
(sc) 10   9   8